Contents

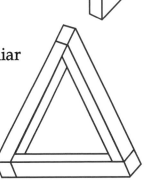

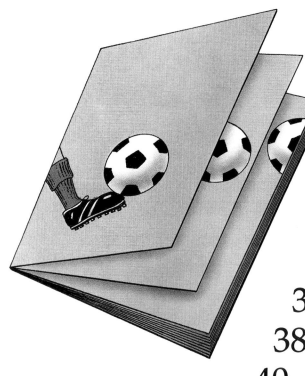

Why See?

All five of your senses are important, but you probably depend on your sight even more than you realise.

SEEING HAS SOME SPECIAL advantages as a way of finding out about your environment. Light bouncing off the things around you reaches your eyes almost instantly, whether the things are close or far away. Unless it's foggy or very dark, you can use your sight to move about quickly and safely. Most animals that make little use of their eyes, and rely on touch and smell, have to move slowly. Seeing can be important even when you are using your other senses. Most people do not develop much sense of touch or smell, but people who lose their sight find that their other senses are full of information. Try the Brain Games below to find out how much information you can obtain without using your eyes.

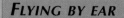

FLYING BY EAR

Bats can fly swiftly and hunt for food in complete darkness. They don't need light or sight; they find their way by listening to the echoes of their own high-pitched squeaks.

Brain Games

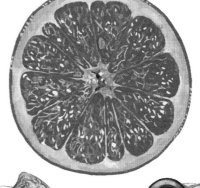

TOUCH TEST

Test your sense of touch. Ask someone to fill some dishes with substances that have different shapes and textures (below). They should do this out of your sight, and without telling you what they are putting in the dishes. They could use pasta shapes, cereals, sweets, bread crumbs, pebbles, buttons, dry leaves, earth, twigs or sawdust. Now, with your eyes closed, try to guess what each one contains by feeling with your fingers.

DO YOU KNOW YOUR FRUIT?

Test your senses of taste and smell. Ask someone to give you pieces of fruit (left) while your eyes are tightly closed. The different fruits should be the same texture — different kinds of berries; grapefruit, lemon and orange; or apple and pear. Taste each one. Can you tell what they are without seeing them? You could also try this with several different fizzy drinks or fruit juices — or different kinds of cheese or chocolate. How well can you tell them apart? Does your sense of taste depend on what your eyes tell you to expect?

SWIMMING BY EAR ▼

Dolphins also have a very sharp sense of hearing which they rely on instead of sight. They make loud squeaks which travel through the water and bounce off any objects nearby. The echoes of the squeaks tell dolphins where things are in the water around them — the fish they eat, dangerous obstacles, or other dolphins. This sense is called echolocation. Sailors in submarines use similar equipment called sonar to locate other ships and explore the ocean floor.

WHAT'S THAT SOUND?

Can you hear what's happening around you (right)? Stand in the middle of a room with your eyes shut (or blindfolded) and ask a friend to move quietly around you, stopping in different places to make noises like crumpling a piece of paper or tapping on a glass. Can you tell what your friend is doing, and where he or she is?

READING BY TOUCH

Write a message on a piece of paper (below) by resting it on a soft surface and pressing hard, so that you can feel ridges on the other side. Make the letters 2–3cm high and write back-to-front so that the message is the right way round on the other side. Now see if a friend can shut their eyes and read it by running their fingers over the raised letters!

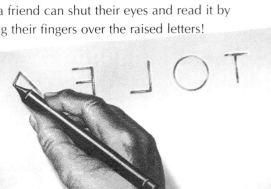

How Your Eyes Work

Your eyes carry out the first vital step in seeing — they form an image of your surroundings.

WHEN YOU SEE something, what happens in your eyes? Light reflected from the object you see passes through the pupil, which is the dark spot in the centre of your iris — the coloured part of your eye. The light hits millions of cells packed together at the back of the eye (the retina). These cells act like electric switches, turning on as light hits them. They send instant messages to the brain with information about the object the eye has seen, such as its colour and distance. An image of the object is formed on the retina and focused by the cornea and the lens. Your lenses adjust to become thicker or thinner, depending on whether you are looking at things close up or in the distance. They become less flexible with age, so most elderly people need glasses. These Brain Games show you some of the ways in which your eyes work.

THE UPSIDE-DOWN IMAGE ▼

The eye's cornea and lens bend rays of light from an object to form an upside-down image of the object on the retina.

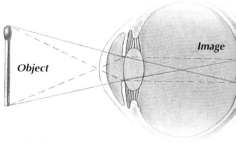

Object

Image

Pupil *The opening through which light passes* ....

Lens *changes shape to focus image on retina* ....

Cornea *protects the lens and assists focusing* ....

Iris *controls the opening of the pupil in response to light* ....

WHO SEES BEST? ▼

All animals with backbones have eyes built in the same way as humans, but seeing is much more important for the survival of some animals than it is for others.

Some small mammals, *such as the shrew hedgehog, have poor eyesight. They rely on their sensitive whiskers and their sense of smell to find food.*

A bird of prey's *ability to pick out detail is 30 times better than ours.*

Primates *need good eyesight to judge distances when leaping through trees.*

A civet *relies more on its sharp hearing and highly developed sense of smell, than on its sense of sight.*

Brain Games

THE SHRINKING PUPIL

The size of your eye's pupil changes automatically depending on how much light is available (below). Cover one eye for several seconds and look in a mirror. Now uncover the eye. See how the pupil grows smaller as it reacts to the extra light coming into the eye.

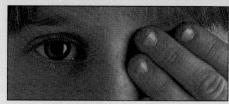

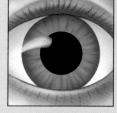

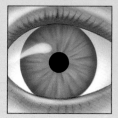

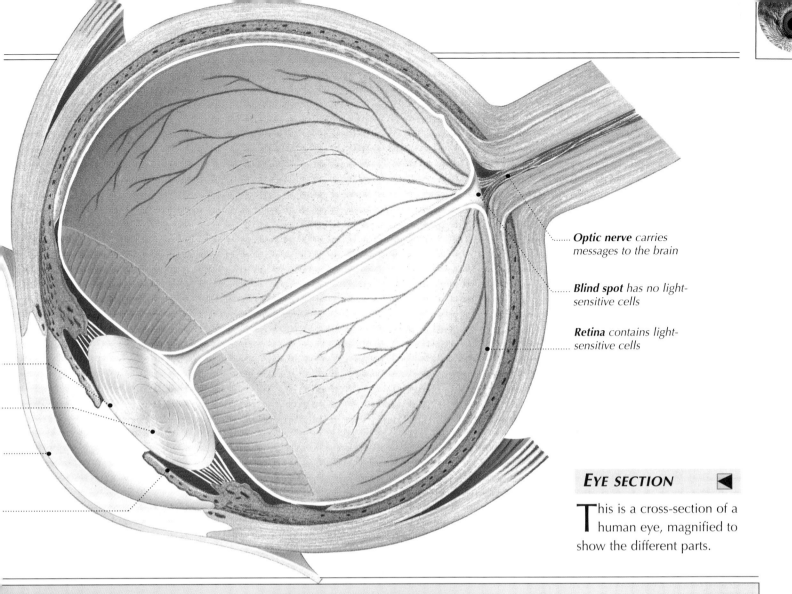

Optic nerve *carries messages to the brain*

Blind spot *has no light-sensitive cells*

Retina *contains light-sensitive cells*

EYE SECTION

This is a cross-section of a human eye, magnified to show the different parts.

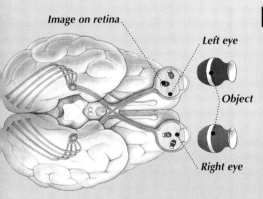

Image on retina

Left eye

Object

Right eye

BINOCULAR VISION

Since your eyes are a little way apart, each sees an object from a slightly different angle (left). The combination of these different views helps you judge an object's distance. Try threading a needle with one eye closed. It's hard to do because without the view from both eyes you cannot judge the distance between the needle and thread accurately.

FIND YOUR BLIND SPOT

Close your left eye and stare at the cross above with your right eye. Hold the book at arm's length and slowly move it towards you until the spot on the right disappears. This happens when light from the spot is focused on your "blind spot", where there are no light-sensitive cells.

FLOATING FINGER

Hold your index fingers about 15 centimetres in front of your eyes, with the tips nearly touching (right). Look between your fingertips and focus on the distance beyond them. You should see a disembodied finger floating in space. This happens because your brain combines the different images from your two eyes.

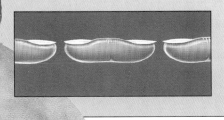

The Adaptable Eye

In order for you to see, your eyes have to keep moving about and adjusting to changing light.

YOUR EYES ARE ALWAYS adjusting so that you can see the world around you. As the light around you grows dim or becomes brighter, the pupils of your eyes expand or contract to let in more light or less, and the cells at the back of your eye automatically turn their sensitivity to light up or down. You can experience this when you go from a dark room into sunlight. At first you are dazzled by the bright light, but only for a minute or so, while your pupils contract and the cells in your eyes turn their sensitivity down.

Your eyes also adjust to your surroundings by moving about, "scanning" different parts of the scene. As you look at this book, your eyes are moving many times a second, picking up details from a little bit of the page at a time. Your brain receives a stream of messages about these little bits, combines them together, and you see the whole page all at once.

VIDEO MIXING ▶

Mixing a video involves watching several TV screens at once. A video editor has to spot when something important happens on a screen, even when they are not looking straight at it. They can do this by keeping their eyes moving all the time, helping them see things out of the corner of their eye. When their eyes stop moving, they can take in the details only of what is in front of them. Everything else is indistinct and may be missed.

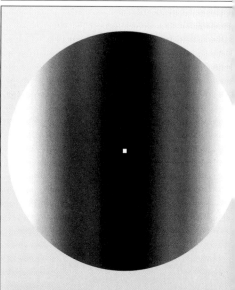

THE FADING BAR

In this picture (above), you can easily see a dark bar with fuzzy edges running down the middle of the circle. Now gaze steadily at the small white dot in the centre of the circle. If you keep your eyes steady enough, the black bar will fade away after 10 seconds or so, and the whole circle will seem to be the same shade. If you move your eyes just a little, the bar will snap back into view again. You can see what a difference it makes to have moveable eyes.

NIGHT VISION ▲

Owls and cats have eyes which are very sensitive to dim light, allowing them to hunt for food at night. Although night vision in humans is not as good, it is still remarkable. Your eyes have 200 million special cells called rods that help you see in the dark. The rods are so sensitive that they can detect the light of a single match lit 80 kilometres away on a perfectly clear, pitch-dark night. They also let you see very well on a dark night deep in the country, with only the moon and stars for light. But rods do not adjust quickly to the dark; they take about 40 minutes to work effectively.

Brain Games

CAN YOU KEEP YOUR EYES STILL?

Stare at the black dot in the middle of the pattern (right) for 30 seconds, without changing your gaze. Now switch your gaze straight to the white dot nearby and stare at it. You will see an "afterimage" — a grid of bright lines crossing the dark squares — which will last for 5 to 10 seconds. The afterimage will jiggle about no matter how hard you try to keep it centred on the white dot. This is because your eyes are always moving slightly, even when you think you are keeping them still.

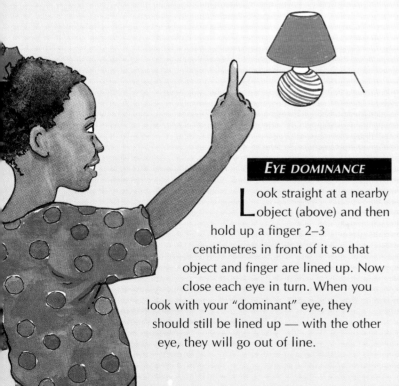

EYE DOMINANCE

Look straight at a nearby object (above) and then hold up a finger 2–3 centimetres in front of it so that object and finger are lined up. Now close each eye in turn. When you look with your "dominant" eye, they should still be lined up — with the other eye, they will go out of line.

READING IN THE DARK

All the letters in this picture (right) are easy to read in bright light. Go into a dark room (not completely dark — there should be some light coming in around the door and curtains). At first, you won't be able to read the letters, but after a few minutes the largest ones should be visible. Wait a bit longer for your eyes to adjust. What is the smallest letter you can see now? What can you see after half an hour?

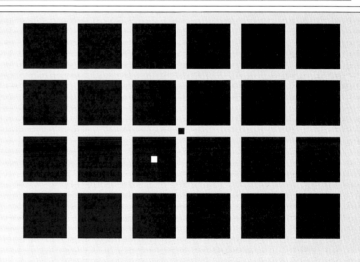

How Much Detail Can You See?

When you look at something, you see a complete picture. You also see small details at the same time.

IMAGINE YOU'RE looking at the outside of your house. You can easily see big parts of it — the roof, the windows, the door — and you can also see small details, like single bricks or a door handle. If you stand very close to the house, you can no longer see all of it. Now imagine walking further away. After a little while you won't be able to make out the small details. The amount of detail you can see is limited by how far away something is. It also depends on whether your vision is properly focused, and whether you look straight at something or out of the corner of your eye.

AERIAL PHOTOGRAPHY ▶

This spy plane can take clear pictures of cities from a height of more than 20 kilometres up in the air. At this distance, roads and houses would no longer be visible to the human eye. The plane is equipped with cameras with special telephoto lenses which "zoom in" to photograph objects too far away to be seen.

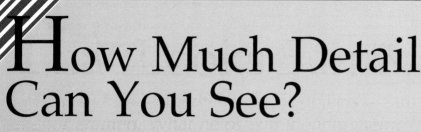

PAINTING WITH DOTS ◀

The artist who painted this picture has created the shapes and colours of people and landscape by using tiny dots of paint of different colours. This style of painting is called "pointillism". It works because people look at the picture from far enough away that they don't notice the fine detail of the dots, but they can see the bigger shapes which the dots make.

Brain Games

STARRY, STARRY NIGHT

Very tiny, faint details are easiest to see if you don't look straight at them! Try this out on a clear, starry night like this (left) by finding a very faint star — it will be easier to see by looking a little to one side of it.

THE SMALL PRINT

One way of printing pictures and photographs (right) is to make them from lots of tiny dots. You can make out the dots with a magnifying glass (a tool for seeing more detail). Try this with pictures from different books, magazines and newspapers. (Try it on words, too!)

THE CORNER OF YOUR EYE

To see detail you need to look straight at something. If you look out of the corner of your eye, you can only make out large shapes. Keep your gaze steady on the spot in the middle of the chart (below), and do not move your eyes. On the right side, you will just be able to make out what all the letters are, but on the left side you will only be able to identify ones close to the spot. The further away something is from the point where your eyes are focused, the bigger it has to be in order for you to make out what it is. We don't usually have this problem because our eyes keep moving all the time.

A U K Z Q • M Y L P K

HORIZONTAL OR VERTICAL?

Try this simple test of your vision for detail. Look at these two patterns (left) from more than six metres away. They will look the same. Now walk towards them. How close do you have to be before you can make out which is vertical and which is horizontal? Try it with one eye, then the other, and compare the results with those of your friends. If you wear glasses or contact lenses, try it without them on.

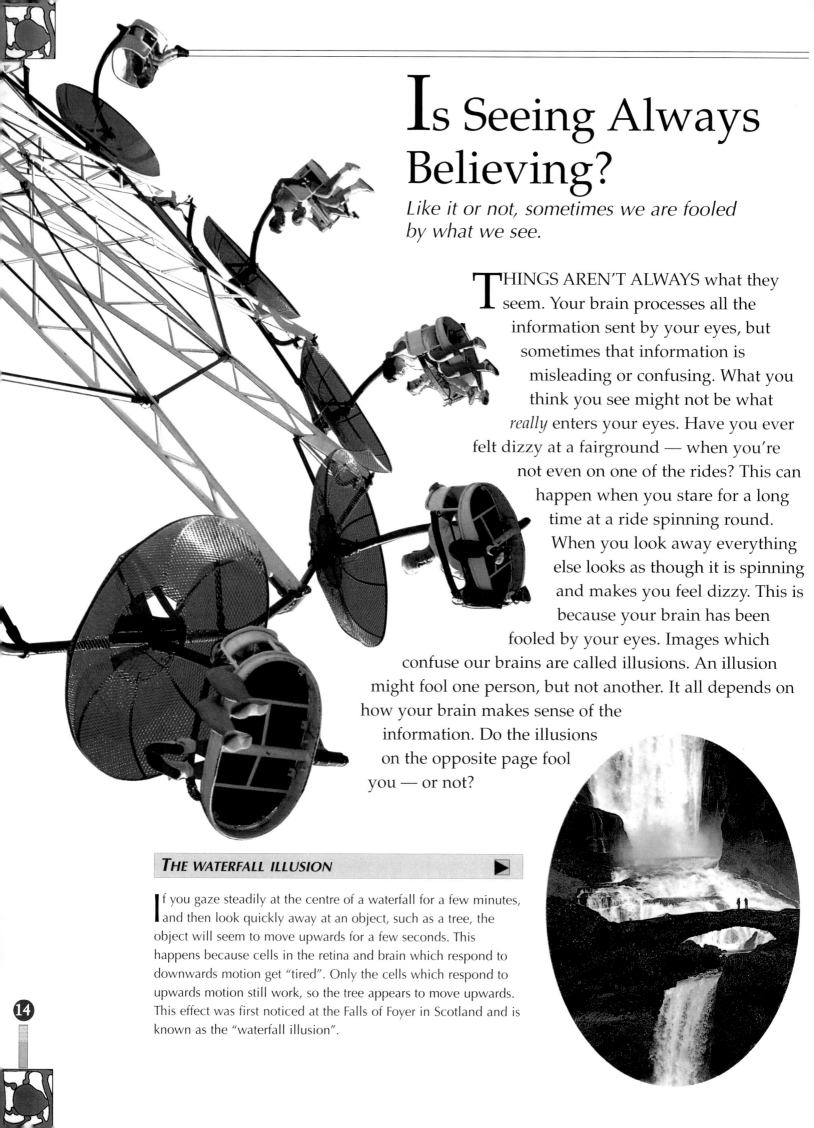

Is Seeing Always Believing?

Like it or not, sometimes we are fooled by what we see.

THINGS AREN'T ALWAYS what they seem. Your brain processes all the information sent by your eyes, but sometimes that information is misleading or confusing. What you think you see might not be what *really* enters your eyes. Have you ever felt dizzy at a fairground — when you're not even on one of the rides? This can happen when you stare for a long time at a ride spinning round. When you look away everything else looks as though it is spinning and makes you feel dizzy. This is because your brain has been fooled by your eyes. Images which confuse our brains are called illusions. An illusion might fool one person, but not another. It all depends on how your brain makes sense of the information. Do the illusions on the opposite page fool you — or not?

THE WATERFALL ILLUSION ▶

If you gaze steadily at the centre of a waterfall for a few minutes, and then look quickly away at an object, such as a tree, the object will seem to move upwards for a few seconds. This happens because cells in the retina and brain which respond to downwards motion get "tired". Only the cells which respond to upwards motion still work, so the tree appears to move upwards. This effect was first noticed at the Falls of Foyer in Scotland and is known as the "waterfall illusion".

Brain Games

WHICH IS BRIGHTER?

The inner circle looks a lighter shade than the ring around it (right). But if you cover the edge of the inner circle with a circular strip of paper about half a centimetre wide, you will see that they are really the same shade. The darker shading around the edge of the inner circle causes the illusion.

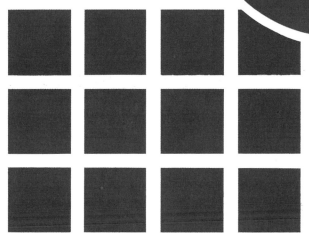

SPOTS BEFORE YOUR EYES

As you look at the grid above, can you see pale grey patches where the white bars cross? They are most visible just to one side of where you are looking, which is why they seem to move as your gaze moves about. The patches are illusions produced by the cells in your retina and brain, which are fooled into combining the bright and dark areas of the picture.

HOW DARK IS IT?

The darkest parts of a TV picture are actually as light as the grey image that is left when you turn the TV off. This is because when the TV is on, pale parts of the picture make other parts seem dark by comparison (right). Try it and see for yourself.

THE WATERFALL ILLUSION ON TV

At the end of a TV programme, stare at the centre of the screen while the credits roll (below). When they stop, the picture will seem to move downwards for a few seconds. Try using a VCR to find out what happens if you play the credits in reverse!

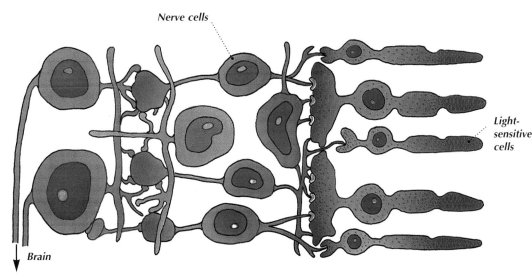

Nerve cells

Light-sensitive cells

Brain

THE RETINAL COMPUTER

The retina at the back of your eye is like a biological microchip. Light-sensitive cells in the retina connect to a network of nerve cells. This network carries out the first computations involved in extracting important information from the retinal image, and sends the results to the brain.

Seeing In Your Head

Mental images are not just for daydreams; they can help when solving problems.

YOU KNOW THE experience of "seeing something that isn't there". It often happens in dreams and daydreams, which seem very real at the time. These pictures in your head are called mental images. They may seem to come from nowhere. But you can make your own mental images just by remembering or imagining something, and you can learn to move and change mental images deliberately as a way of solving puzzles. This skill — called visualisation — seems to be a special talent, very different from intelligence. Some people have good visualisation skills, while others, who are equally intelligent, do not.

ARTIST AT WORK ▶

Artists, like this caricaturist, need good powers of mental imagery. They have to be able to picture the finished work in their heads, as they may want it to look quite different from what they can actually see.

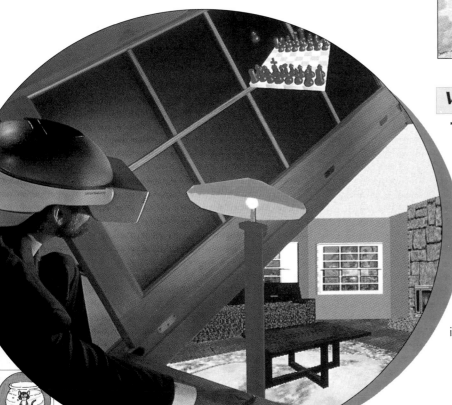

VIRTUAL REALITY ◀

This architect is using a virtual reality system in which miniature TV screens are built into the goggles. The imaginary scene on the screen changes as he turns his head or walks. You may know about virtual reality from playing computer games. When you move a "mouse", or press arrow keys on a keyboard, the picture on the screen changes as if you were moving through a real scene. Virtual reality is useful to engineers and architects as a way of bringing their mental images to life without building expensive models. They can design a car or a building and then use a virtual reality system to "move" around it and inside it, and see what it looks like from any direction.

Brain Games

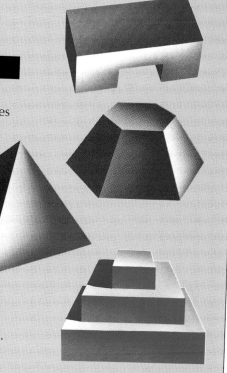

Look at the picture on the left. The artist has made eight mistakes in drawing the scene. Can you find them? (Check the Answers page when you think you have found all of them.) This puzzle tests your ability to see or visualise how shapes should look compared with how they have been drawn. If you found all of the mistakes quickly, you are probably good at drawing.

IMAGERY AND MEMORY

You can use mental imagery to remember a list. One way is to imagine funny pictures (below) of things you want to remember, such as weekend tasks (hand-washing a woolly jumper, doing homework, feeding the fish, and having friends to tea). This method can also help you remember shopping lists or facts for exams.

COMPLETE THE PICTURE

The picture below just seems to be a lot of black and white patches. But keep looking at it, and you should see something familiar. (If you can't, look at the Answers page.) When you've seen it once, or know what to look for, the object is easy to see, because you can form a mental image to help you find it.

COUNTING SIDES

How well can you use mental imagery? Look at each of the four shapes above, and count how many sides each shape has (not just the ones you can see, but the ones out of sight as well). To do this, you have to "turn" the object around in your mind and imagine seeing it from other directions. Check your results on the Answers page.

Objects And Backgrounds

All by itself, your brain has learnt complicated rules for telling objects and backgrounds apart.

AN IMAGE OF A SCENE in front of you falls on the retina at the back of your eye. The image is broken down by the millions of light-sensitive cells in your retina, each cell responding to the colour and brightness of the light in a tiny patch of the image. But instead of seeing a confusing jumble of the patches of light, you see separate objects standing out against a background. Your brain knows that "objects" are things that are surrounded, and that "backgrounds" are the surrounding space. It also knows that the patterns covering the surface of an object have different shapes, colours and sizes from those covering the background. This helps it to separate the two. You can see how your brain does all this by trying these games in which it is sometimes difficult to tell objects and backgrounds apart.

Brain Games

FLOATING RECTANGLE

When you look at this drawing (below), what you see appears to be a rectangle floating above the page. But now look carefully at the gaps between the circles. The edges of the rectangle that you expect to see aren't actually there. Your brain has automatically linked together the shaded parts of the circles to give the illusion of a rectangle.

GOING DOTTY

Are the red dots (right) grouped horizontally or vertically? How about the green dots and the blue dots (below)? The rows of red dots could be grouped either way, because they are evenly spaced. Wider spaces divide the green dots into four clear rows. The blue dots can easily be grouped by their colours.

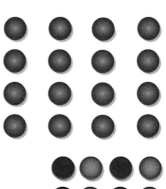

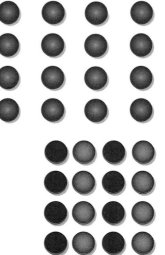

SPIRAL ILLUSION

When you look at this drawing, you immediately see a spiral pattern standing out against a chequered background. But now try to trace the spiral with your finger. It isn't there! The short curved lines really make circles. Your brain, confused by the background, mistakenly links the short lines and interprets them as a foreground image — the nonexistent spiral.

SKULL OR DRINKERS?

When you first look at this picture, you probably see a skull. But keep looking, especially around the "eyes" and "teeth" — can you see two people leaning towards each other over a table covered in glasses? Once you do, you'll find that you can flip backwards and forwards between seeing one thing or the other — though you won't be able to see both at once! Your brain is jumping between deciding that the two big dark patches are part of the background of the skull, or part of the foreground of the scene with the two drinkers.

WHICH IS THE PROPELLER?

In these figures (right), do you see a green propeller against a white background, or do you see a white propeller against a green background? Which of these pictures makes it easiest to see a white propeller? Try making your own drawings to find out what happens with different propeller sizes.

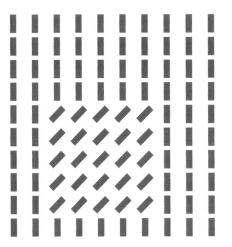

FIND THE SQUARE

The two grids (left) both contain a square made from pieces that contrast with the rest. The square in the far-left grid "jumps out" at you, but can you find the one in the near-left grid? Small differences between the pieces of a picture sometimes stand out immediately. But this doesn't always happen, and we may have to search for the differences. (See the Answers page.)

Nature's Illusions

To survive, many animals have evolved to look like their backgrounds, or like something else entirely! Some disguises can fool human experts as well as the animal's enemies or prey.

FOR MOST ANIMALS, keeping out of the way of predators is a matter of life and death. If its predators hunt by vision, then an animal will have a better chance of surviving if it is hard to see against its background. For predators, it is easier to capture prey if the prey can't see them coming. This is the simple reason for animal camouflage, but there are as many kinds of camouflage as there are animals. Some camouflaged animals have the same colour and texture as their background. This allows them to blend into the scenery even if they are as big as polar bears. Others have markings that seem to attract attention but actually make them harder to see. Others resemble things that are inedible or poisonous.

STANDING OUT TO BLEND IN ▼

Some animals are covered in markings that make the outline of their whole body harder to see. This is called disruptive coloration. The black and white stripes of a zebra look conspicuous to us, but in fact they provide a very effective form of camouflage. When a group of zebras are together, the confusing patterns of the stripes make it difficult for a lion or other predator to pick out a single target for attack.

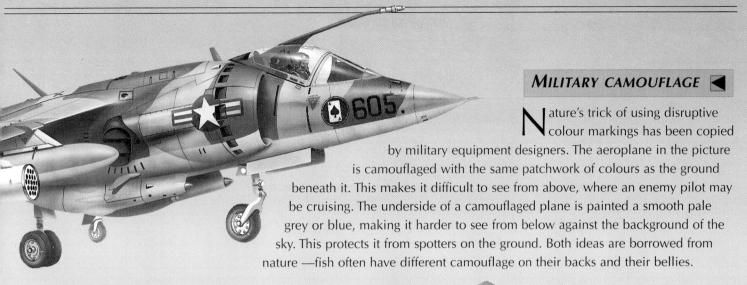

Nature's trick of using disruptive colour markings has been copied by military equipment designers. The aeroplane in the picture is camouflaged with the same patchwork of colours as the ground beneath it. This makes it difficult to see from above, where an enemy pilot may be cruising. The underside of a camouflaged plane is painted a smooth pale grey or blue, making it harder to see from below against the background of the sky. This protects it from spotters on the ground. Both ideas are borrowed from nature —fish often have different camouflage on their backs and their bellies.

Brain Games

FIND THE ANIMALS

In the imaginary underwater scene on the left, there are 18 camouflaged marine animals. See how many you can find among the rocks, sand and seaweed. Turn to the Answers page to check if you are right. Would you make a good underwater predator? (If you were a predator, you would probably be camouflaged yourself!)

FALSE IDENTITY

Look at the pictures below and try to decide what an animal would think each one is. With this form of camouflage, animals protect themselves by appearing to be something they are not — something which does not interest their predators. Turn to the Answers page to find out what they are.

Colour

To see colours, our eyes and brains must respond differently to different kinds of light rays.

THE LIGHT THAT comes from the sun or an electric light is made up of light rays with different wavelengths. Under white or natural light, objects of different colours absorb some of these wavelengths and reflect only the wavelength of the colour you see. In other words, a banana absorbs all the wavelengths except yellow, so it appears yellow to your eyes. Most people's eyes have three kinds of light receptors (cones), and each works best in light of a different wavelength: short, medium or long, for blue, green and red. These are the primary (main) colours of light. White light — "pure" light — is made up of all the wavelengths or colours together.

PRISMS

A prism is a specially cut piece of glass that "splits" white light into all the colours of the spectrum. It does this by bending some wavelengths more than others. The long wavelengths are bent the least; when they fall on a white screen, it looks red. The short wavelengths are bent the most, and they look violet. The whole sequence of colours in the spectrum is red, orange, yellow, green, blue, indigo and violet. Light with wavelengths outside this range is invisible to human eyes (but not to some animals). If its wavelength is longer than red light, it is called infrared; if the wavelength is shorter than violet light, it is called ultraviolet.

WHY SEE IN COLOUR?

Seeing in colour helps animals to survive in their natural environments. Many animals feed on fruits, nuts and berries, and it can be difficult to spot these quickly in a large mass of leaves. Colour vision makes it easier, because the animal can see the difference between the leaves and the fruit. The greater the contrast, the easier it is to see the fruit. Can you think of some things that would be more difficult for you to do if you couldn't see in colour?

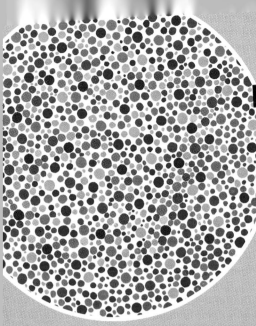

Brain Games

COLOUR BLINDNESS

Can you see a number in the pattern of dots on the left? Don't worry if you cannot — lots of people are red-green colour blind, which means only that they can't tell some colours apart because their eyes have only two kinds of cones instead of three. About four percent of all people are colour blind — mostly males. (The answer is on the Answers page.)

NEGATIVE AFTERIMAGES

Stare at the centre of the cross in the blue circle (above) for 20 seconds, then look at the dot in the grey square. Let your eyes recover, then repeat the steps with the yellow circle and the grey square. What did you see? These brief "afterimages" appear in the complementary colour to the colour you stared at. (Complementary colours produce white light when mixed.) Yellow and blue are complementary, and so are green and magenta (a dark purple-red). You see afterimages because the cells carrying messages from your eyes to your brain take time to adjust to a new colour after seeing the same colour for a while.

COLOUR AFTERIMAGES

Look at the black and white pattern below — there are no colours in it. Now stare at the red lines on the right for 10 seconds, then at the green lines in the middle for 10 seconds. Keep repeating this for at least three minutes (5–10 minutes if you have enough patience). When you've finished, look at the black and white pattern again. What colour are the lines now? Your brain has linked the direction of the lines with their colour. Look at the black and white pattern again an hour later, and the pale "afterimage" colours will probably still be there!

COLOURS AND BACKGROUNDS

In the squares on the right are four colours against two different backgrounds, black and white. Look carefully at each pair of coloured squares, one at a time. Are they the same colour, or does one row look brighter? The colours you see aren't just a matter of the wavelengths of light bouncing off objects. Your brain is also influenced by the colours in the surrounding area. In this case, the colours look much more vivid with a black background than with a white one.

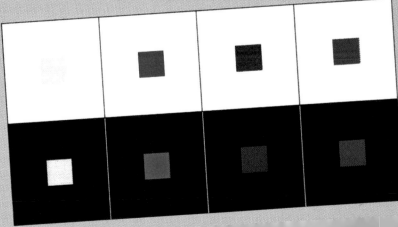

Seeing In Colour

What colours you can see depends on light-sensitive cells in your eyes. The same is true for animals.

MANY ANIMALS SEE COLOURS, but they may see them in different ways. Birds, bees, cats and humans, for example, have different colour vision because they have different kinds of eyes. Their eyes all have special cells called cones that "see" colour — they are sensitive to different wavelengths of light. Cats' and dogs' eyes have only two kinds of cones. This means that they can't distinguish some colours which humans can. Birds have four or more different sorts of cone, so two different berries might look the same colour to you, but they look very different to a blackbird. Many animals have cones sensitive to ultraviolet light, which is invisible to humans. For bees, the three primary colours detected by their cones are green, blue and ultraviolet.

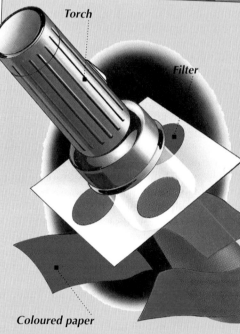

Torch

Filter

Coloured paper

INDOORS AND OUTDOORS ▲

Ordinary cameras cannot adjust for changes in the colour of light, and you have to use different film for taking pictures in daylight and in artificial light. Both these pictures were taken with the same daylight film — the outdoor scene looks normal, but the indoor one has far too much red and orange in it. This is because the light from an electric lightbulb has more red wavelengths, and less blue wavelengths, than sunlight. Your brain adjusts to this difference automatically — if it didn't, a piece of white paper would look slightly blue in daylight and orange under electric light! Your brain can't compensate perfectly, though, which explains why it is sometimes difficult to choose the colour of clothes or paint under artificial light.

COLOUR CONSTANCY

You will need a torch (above), a piece of white card, and some flat pieces of coloured plastic. You also need some squares of unpatterned coloured paper and a colourful picture. Make a filter for the torch by cutting circles in the white card and putting a piece of plastic at the back of each circle. In a very dark room, look at the squares one by one under the coloured light, beginning with a pale filter (such as yellow). What happens to the squares? Now look at the picture under the same filter. Does the same thing happen? When you see many colours at once, your brain compensates for the torch light and the colours look the same as in normal light.

BEE VISION

Bees feed on nectar from flowers, and they need to be able to tell from a distance which flowers are worth visiting. They do this by spotting the pattern of colours on the petals. Because the light-sensitive cells in a bee's eye are different from ours, colour patterns on petals may look very different to you and to a bee. Some flowers have petals that look pure white to humans; but there are patches on these petals that reflect different amounts of ultraviolet light. So to a bee, they have very obvious dark markings, making them easy to tell apart.

Brain Games

FLOWER SHOW

During the spring or summer, try this simple experiment on bees' colour vision. Cut out flower shapes (below) from thin card of different colours. (Make sure you use at least red, yellow, green and blue.) Put a plastic bottle cap full of sugared water in the centres. Find a clump of real flowers which is being visited by lots of bees, and arrange the cardboard flowers nearby. Watch patiently. Bees will land on the cardboard flowers to investigate. Count how many visits each one gets. Which is the bees' favourite colour?

COLOURED DOTS

At normal reading distance, the red, blue and black dots on the left are easy to tell apart. Now prop up the book at slightly more than arm's length away and look again. The red dots stand out clearly, but it is harder to tell which are black and which are blue. This is because the light receptors in your eyes that are sensitive to blue are thinly scattered over the back of your retina, and so it is harder to tell blue from black in the small details of a pattern seen at a distance.

MAKE YOUR OWN RAINBOW

When sun shines through raindrops, the raindrops break up the light in the same way that a prism does, making a rainbow. You can make your own rainbow (right) by putting a glass of water on a window sill in bright sunlight, with the glass slightly over the edge of the sill. Put a large sheet of white paper on the floor below the window, and you will see a rainbow pattern of colours falling on it.

Seeing In Depth

When your brain combines the messages from your two eyes, it helps you see a solid world — one with depth.

WHEN SCIENTISTS FIRST DISCOVERED how our eyes work, they were puzzled by many things. Why did the world look solid, even though the images formed on the retina at the back of the eye were flat? How did people make out shapes, and tell how far away they were? We now know that it helps to have two eyes, which give us binocular vision. The right eye and the left eye have a slightly different view of the world, forming different images on the retina. The closer you are to something, the more different it looks to each of your eyes. Our ability to know where things are in relation to us is called depth perception, and it helps us to see a solid world. Some of the Brain Games opposite show how flat pictures can be made to look solid if you look at different parts of the pictures with each eye. In infancy, our brains become "wired up" to combine the messages from the two eyes. About five percent of people will not be able to see the effects here.

THE CIRCLING PENDULUM

Make a pendulum (above) with a lump of plasticine or rubber hanging from a length of cotton, and s it swinging back and forth across your line of vision. If you put one lens of a pair of dark glasses in front of one of your eyes, the pendulum will seem to circle, swinging alternately nearer and further from you as it goes back and forth. Take the dark glasses away, and you will see that it is really still swingi straight! The pendulum appears to mov in a circle because the dark glass slow down the messages to one of your eye

SEEING DOUBLE

Look steadily at an object about an arm's length away. Now hold a pencil upright and move it back and forth between the object and your nose, always keeping your gaze on th object. At a certain point you will notice that the pencil magically becomes two pencils.

FLAT OR SOLID? ▶

When you look at the moon, you see a flat disc, although it is really a solid sphere. This is because the moon is too far away for there to be any noticeable difference between its images in each of your eyes; and without slightly different images in each eye, you cannot see it has depth. Your eyes would have to be several thousand kilometres apart to see the moon as solid! A powerful lens was used for this picture.

Brain Games

BEHIND THE SCENE

Hold this picture (left) so that it touches your nose. Let your eyes relax, and stare "through the picture" into space. Now move the page slowly to arm's length, still staring through it all the time. After a few tries, you should see a hidden object in the design. Can you tell what it is? (See the Answers page if you are not sure.)

COMBINING TWO IMAGES

Stare at a point between the two drawings (right), trying to look "through the page" into the distance. At first, you'll just see double images, but if you are patient you may be able to make the two images come together in the middle, and see a solid object coming out of the page towards you.

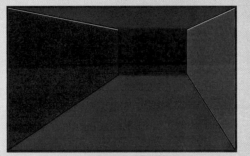

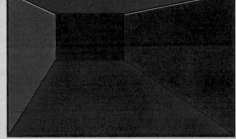

Left eye view

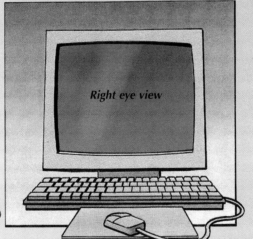

Right eye view

JUMPING OBJECTS

Look at an object nearby such as a computer (left). Open one eye and close the other, over and over. The object seems to jump from side to side. Things closer to you jump more than things further away, because up close there is more difference between the view in each eye.

3-D THRILLS ▶

In some sci-fi and horror films of the 1950s, monsters seemed to burst out of the screen at the audience. This trick was set up by taking two films from slightly different angles, printing one in red and one in green, and having audiences look at them with a red filter over one eye and a green filter over the other. Each eye sees just one of the pictures, and the scene appears solid.

Depth And Perspective

The rules of perspective used in drawing help us to understand the layout of things around us.

YOUR BRAIN COMBINES the information from your two eyes about the relative size and positions of parts of what you are looking at to enable you to judge distances. For instance, when you walk down a street, your eyes pass information to your brain about the cars, people and buildings so you don't bump into things.

Until about 500 years ago, artists did not know how to show distance in their paintings. Pictures tended to look flat and lacking in depth. Then the rules of perspective were discovered — rules of drawing which enabled artists to give their pictures depth. Now they could draw a road winding into the distance or a person's arm reaching towards you. These rules are still used today. Try the Brain Games to find out more about perspective.

A FLAT WORLD ▲

Artists in ancient Egypt painted this scene thousands of years ago, before the rules of perspective were discovered. The figures look flat, and the scene has no depth.

IMPOSSIBLE PICTURE

Here is an amazing picture (left) in which the normal rules of perspective are not being used correctly, making it an "impossible" scene. How many things can you find wrong with the picture? There are at least 10 to look for. When you think you have found them all, turn to the Answers page to see if you are right.

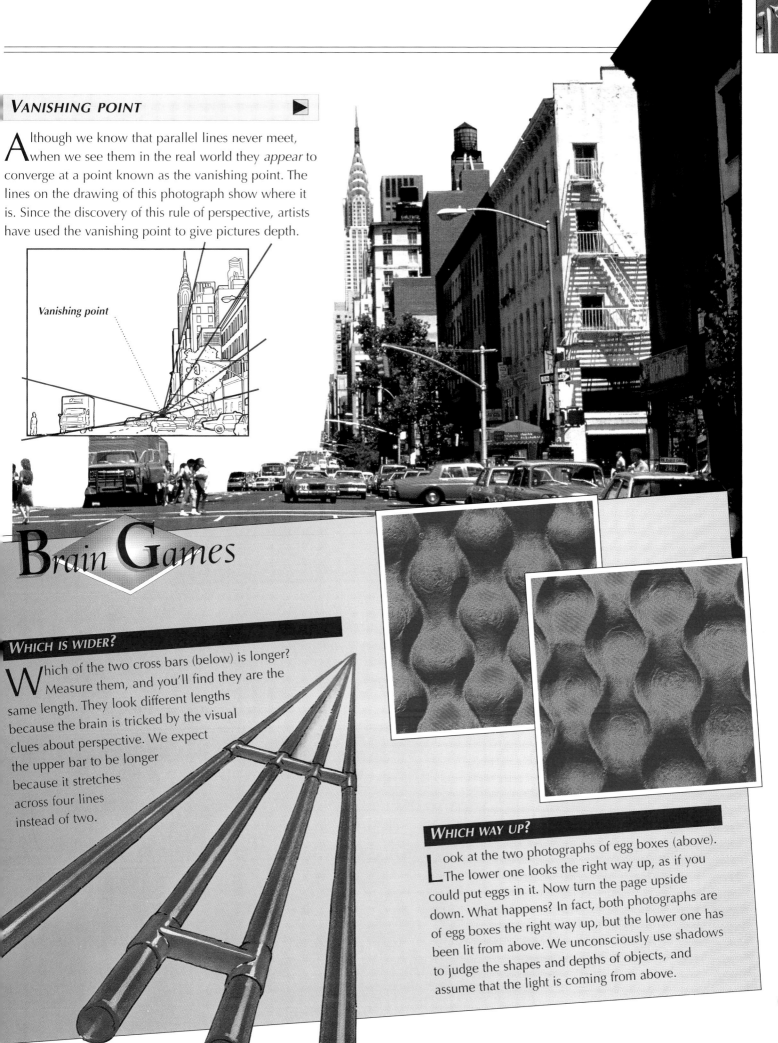

VANISHING POINT ▶

Although we know that parallel lines never meet, when we see them in the real world they *appear* to converge at a point known as the vanishing point. The lines on the drawing of this photograph show where it is. Since the discovery of this rule of perspective, artists have used the vanishing point to give pictures depth.

Vanishing point

Brain Games

WHICH IS WIDER?

Which of the two cross bars (below) is longer? Measure them, and you'll find they are the same length. They look different lengths because the brain is tricked by the visual clues about perspective. We expect the upper bar to be longer because it stretches across four lines instead of two.

WHICH WAY UP?

Look at the two photographs of egg boxes (above). The lower one looks the right way up, as if you could put eggs in it. Now turn the page upside down. What happens? In fact, both photographs are of egg boxes the right way up, but the lower one has been lit from above. We unconsciously use shadows to judge the shapes and depths of objects, and assume that the light is coming from above.

Seeing Things Move

Your eyes depend on your brain to interpret moving objects. This is more difficult if you are moving too.

WHEN THINGS MOVE around you, their images on the backs of your eyes move too. Your brain is able to work out from these changing images what is moving, how fast it is moving and in what direction. It can do this quickly enough for you to rollerskate, dodge a snowball or play a computer game. Sometimes your brain can be tricked, so that you see movement when there really is none, or you see the wrong thing move. There are even times when your brain tells you that you are moving, even though you are still. This happens when everything around you moves but your brain assumes that the movement of the image on the eye has happened because it is you that is moving.

WHICH IS MOVING? ▼

When you look at a small object against a bigger background, your brain assumes that the background is always still. If there is any movement, it seems to be the object and not the background that is moving. Usually this is right, but not always! On a windy night when clouds are blowing across the sky, look at the moon as the clouds pass in front of it. It will look as if the moon is racing past the clouds.

ANIMATION ▼

As you watch a film, you see the picture move. You are actually being shown one slightly different still picture after another. Because they change 24 times a second, you don't see each one disappear and then another one appear. Instead, you see a continuously moving scene. Special high-speed film is needed to show movement in still pictures like these.

Brain Games

THE MOVING DOT

Cover the end of a torch (right) with dark tape. Prop it on a table to keep it still, and make a tiny hole in the tape with a pin. Stare at the dot of light from across a completely dark room, keeping your head still. What happens to the dot? Your brain is tricked into seeing it move because your eyes continue to move slightly in the dark.

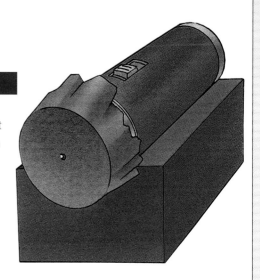

PUT THE FISH IN THE BOWL

Draw a fish on one piece of card and a bowl of water on another (left). Fasten the edges of the cards together with the pictures facing out. Leave enough room to attach a thin stick or a pencil firmly in the centre. Spin the stick rapidly. Because your brain sees both sides at once, the fish jumps into the bowl!

MAKE YOUR OWN CARTOON

To see how animation works, try making a simple cartoon (above). You will need a pad of paper that you can shuffle through quickly with your thumb (either a notepad or some unruled index cards stapled together at the far edge will do). On each sheet, draw a simple object such as a small circle a little higher each time, then a little lower and so on. Now shuffle the pad. What do you see?

OLD-FASHIONED HOME MOVIES

Start with a strip of cardboard about 96cm long and 12cm high. Draw a series of pictures like the ones shown below along the strip, and cut slits in the sides (be careful not to cut the pictures!). Fold the strip into a circle and make a matching cardboard circle to put underneath it. Attach the strip to the circle and paint the outside black. Put a pin through the centre of the circle and attach it to a cork. Put the cork in a bottle for stability, and stand it under a light. To see the action, spin the disc and look through the slits.

Light from lamp

Pin with cork attached underneath the card

Optical Illusions

Optical illusions trick your brain into making wrong conclusions. Here are some ways to create them.

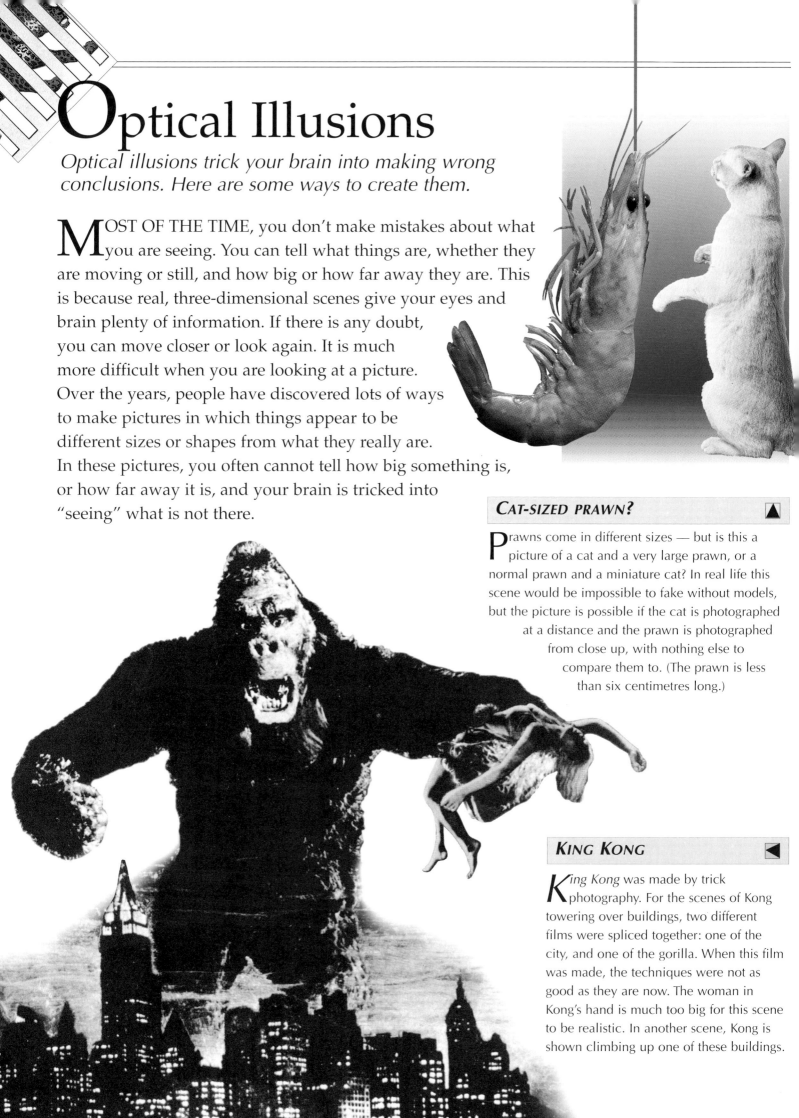

MOST OF THE TIME, you don't make mistakes about what you are seeing. You can tell what things are, whether they are moving or still, and how big or how far away they are. This is because real, three-dimensional scenes give your eyes and brain plenty of information. If there is any doubt, you can move closer or look again. It is much more difficult when you are looking at a picture. Over the years, people have discovered lots of ways to make pictures in which things appear to be different sizes or shapes from what they really are. In these pictures, you often cannot tell how big something is, or how far away it is, and your brain is tricked into "seeing" what is not there.

CAT-SIZED PRAWN?

Prawns come in different sizes — but is this a picture of a cat and a very large prawn, or a normal prawn and a miniature cat? In real life this scene would be impossible to fake without models, but the picture is possible if the cat is photographed at a distance and the prawn is photographed from close up, with nothing else to compare them to. (The prawn is less than six centimetres long.)

KING KONG

King Kong was made by trick photography. For the scenes of Kong towering over buildings, two different films were spliced together: one of the city, and one of the gorilla. When this film was made, the techniques were not as good as they are now. The woman in Kong's hand is much too big for this scene to be realistic. In another scene, Kong is shown climbing up one of these buildings.

Brain Games

SPINNING DISC

Draw two circles each about 9 centimetres across (left) close together on a piece of card, then draw two pictures in the circles like the ones shown here. (One of them must be upside-down.) Cut the circles out, leaving them joined in the centre, and glue them back to back to make a disc. Make two holes at opposite edges of the disc. Cut two pieces of string 40 centimetres long. Thread one string through each hole and knot its ends together. Twist the strings rapidly between your fingers to spin the disc. The drawings on each side of the disc seem to combine together into a complete picture!

MOVING W

Fold a rectangular sheet of paper (right) into four equal lengths and stand it on a table in a W shape. Keeping your head still, look at it with one eye shut and try to make it "reverse", so that the two corners marked with dots in the picture seem to be at the top of the shape, not on the table. (This may take a while!) Once you can keep the shape reversed, move your head slowly — you will see the piece of paper twist and turn as you move. This happens because your brain interprets the moving image on your eye wrongly.

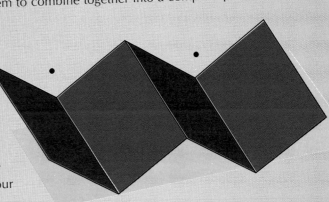

REVERSING ARROW

Draw an arrow facing right on a piece of paper (below) and prop it upright on a table. Place a glass full of water in front of it, stand back a little and look at the arrow through the glass. Which way is it facing now? This optical illusion happens because rays of light are bent before they reach your eye. Other illusions happen for the same kind of reason. For example, when a road looks shiny on a hot day, what you are really seeing is the sky reflected by a layer of hot air!

OPTICAL ZOO-LUSION

This is a double drawing (below). As it is shown here, the top section looks like a very strange jumble. But if you put the bars over the jumbled drawing and slide them from side to side, you will see two completely different animals in turn. To make this "moving zoo" optical illusion work, carefully trace the bars onto a piece of thick paper, making them exactly the same size as they are here. Then cut out the spaces between the bars. Last of all, fit the bars over the picture and slide them back and forth. What two animals do you see in the cage?

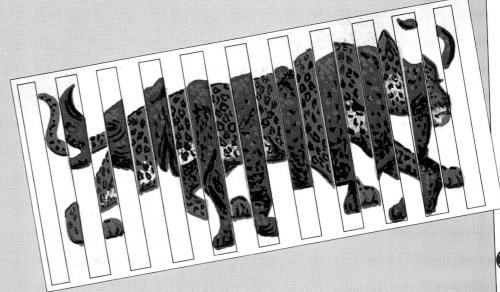

Geometric Illusions

Optical illusions can also play tricks when you look at simple shapes.

SOME ILLUSIONS work by not giving you complete information about a scene. Others work by giving two or more sets of information that seem to match up until you look closely! This is often more obvious in geometric shapes. When you try to judge the length of a line in a drawing, or the size of an angle, your brain is influenced by other parts of the drawing and it is impossible to make yourself see only the part you need to see. Designers learn this. When in doubt, they check length with a ruler.

WHICH WAY IS UP? ▶

A journey through this "House of Stairs" is difficult to make, because the stairs don't let you go anywhere. The artist plays tricks with perspective and creates a scene that looks realistic until you try to join up the different parts by following the stairs.

IMPOSSIBLE SHAPES ▼

The two drawings below are simpler examples of "impossible" shapes. They seem to be three-dimensional shapes. When you look at them more closely, you can see that the lines do not join up as they ought to. Actually, the shapes are flat (two-dimensional), but your brain tries to make them three-dimensional as if they were real objects.

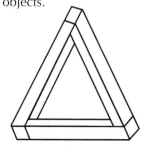

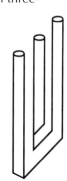

Brain Games

WHICH IS TALLER?

Is the corner of the room taller than the corner of the building (below)? Measure them both with a ruler. (Measure all the way to the carpet.) The room seems taller because the angles at the top and bottom seem to open out, drawing your eye with them.

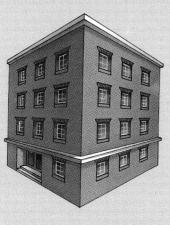

MAKE A SLIDE RULE

Fold a piece of card in half lengthways and tape the long edge closed to form a tube (right). On one side, draw a two-headed arrow measuring 6cm between the arrow points, with one point touching one end of the tube. On the back, draw a scale measuring exactly 6cm, with one end touching the same end as the arrow on the other side. Now take another piece of card of the same width and draw another arrow exactly 6cm long, but with only one arrow — this one pointing in. On the back, mark off 6cm as if on a ruler. Put the second piece into the tube and ask a friend to slide it back and forth to try to make the two arrow figures the same length. Turn the tube over to check their judgment.

CIRCLE CONFUSION

Look at the circle pattern on the right. Are the two horizontal lines parallel, or do they seem to bend away from the centre of the circle? Now check them with a ruler. You'll find that they don't actually bend, but are really straight and parallel to one another! Here, your impression of the shape of the lines is influenced by the pattern in the background, even after you know from using a ruler that the lines are really straight. Try drawing your own patterns. What kinds of background make the straight lines appear to bend?

A PERFECT SQUARE?

Is the shape in the middle of the picture (below) a square, with all four sides equal and right angles at its corners? Once you have decided, check your answer by measuring the lengths of the sides with a ruler. Now compare the angles with the corners of a rectangular sheet of paper. This illusion happens because the background pattern of lines makes you see the square in a different way. Your brain guesses that the square is standing upright on a flat surface, and uses the rules of perspective to interpret its shape.

BENT OR STRAIGHT?

Look at the figure below. Is the diagonal line straight, or is it slightly bent? When you are sure of the answer, check with a ruler. The rectangle that "interrupts" the line is what causes this illusion.

Memory Games

Images are thought to be much easier to remember than words or numbers. How good is your visual memory?

YOUR BRAIN keeps memories of what the world around you looks like. Usually, you don't realise that you're doing this, because a stream of new information is coming in from your eyes all the time. But if the lights go out, or you close your eyes, you have to rely on your memory to know where things are around you, to pick something up or to stop yourself from tripping over. All these memories are stored as pictures in your brain. There are many kinds of games you can play to find out more about your memory. The easiest things to remember are the ones you are most interested in.

PHOTOGRAPHIC MEMORY

Some people have a "photographic memory"— they can remember lots of details about things that they have seen only once. To test your memory for details, look at the picture above for a few minutes. Then turn to the Answers page and try to answer the questions about this picture without looking back at this page. How well do you do?

NUMBERS AND MEMORY

Look at one row of numbers below. Wait a minute, then without looking at it, try to write it down. Now try the other number, but first break it down into shorter sections. You should find this much easier! Now try memorising a new number that a friend has made up and read aloud. Do your eyes remember better than your ears?

14921793
01738526

DONKEY WORK ▲

When you play "Pin the tail on the donkey", you have to remember exactly where the donkey is so that when your eyes are covered, you can walk in the right direction and reach out to pin the tail in the right place. The player is usually turned round and round a few times after being blindfolded, because this makes it harder to remember the direction in which you have to go. What else do you think might make the donkey harder to find? Test out your ideas next time you play the game.

Brain Games

TEST ON A TRAY

Play the game below to test your own and your friends' memories. Put a collection of common objects on a tray and show it to a friend for five seconds. Then ask them to shut their eyes and name as many of the objects as they can. Count how many they get right, and then swap round and try it yourself with a new set of objects. Who gets the highest score? What happens if you are distracted while you are trying to remember? After you close your eyes, try multiplying two-digit numbers in your head before saying what was on the tray. How much does your score go down?

CARD SHARP

Spread out a pack of playing cards (above) face down. Take turns to turn two cards over, letting the other players see them. If the cards have the same value (for example, two nines or two jacks), you keep them and score a point. If they don't, put them back, face down. The game lasts until all the cards are matched in pairs. The winner has the most pairs.

WHAT DID YOU SEE?

How good are you at remembering exactly what something looks like? Look at the two drawings below for a few seconds. Wait a few minutes, then turn to the Answers page where you will see six drawings. Only two of them are identical to the ones below. Can you tell which ones they are without looking back at this page?

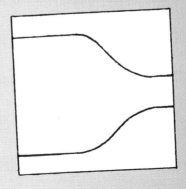
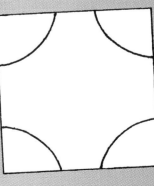

Standing Up Straight

Whether you are doing acrobatics or just standing up straight, seeing helps you keep your balance.

WHEN YOU ARE AWAKE, even when you are doing something as simple as standing up straight, your brain is keeping control of the positions of your body and your limbs. You're not usually aware that this is going on. You may be putting all your mental energy into talking to a friend, and have no idea that you are having to do anything at all to keep upright. But all the time your brain is monitoring your balance and sending commands to muscles in your legs and body to keep you upright. One way your brain does this is through vision. The tiny movements of the images on your eyes, caused when you sway slightly, are enough to set off a reaction in your muscles to stop you falling over.

AN UPSIDE-DOWN WORLD ▶

Imagine the world looked upside-down, and "left" became "right" — would you be able to pick things up, walk through doors, or climb stairs? At first you would be totally confused, but after several days your brain would adjust and you would start to see things the right way up again! One real-life situation in which people learn to cope when they actually are upside down is when a fighter pilot learns to fly an aeroplane while looking at an upside-down world. Many people become dizzy or ill if they are upside-down. Pilots must learn to tolerate it.

WALKING A TIGHTROPE ▼

As toddlers, we all had to learn how to use our senses of sight and balance to stand upright and to walk, suffering a few bruises along the way. Older children and adults can learn to control their balance even more accurately. When acrobats perform amazing feats of balance, such as walking on a tightrope, or standing on one leg on the back of a moving horse, they are using vision to control their balance in basically the same way as you do when you stand up.

DOING A PIROUETTE

How do ballet dancers and ice skaters keep their balance when they spin round and round? The trick is to fix your gaze on one point as long as you can, then snap your head round at the last minute. Try twirling a few times along the length of a room — you'll feel less dizzy if you use this trick and will be able to control your balance!

Brain Games

WHERE ARE YOUR HANDS?

Stretch your arms out in front of you with your thumbs out, an inch or so apart. Now close your eyes, raise one arm above your head, and bring it back down so that your thumbs feel level. Now open your eyes. Are they where you thought they were?

BALANCE ON ONE LEG

Because you are used to standing up, your brain can monitor your balance when you stand up with your eyes closed. But what happens when you try to stand in an unusual posture like the one in the picture (right)? Compare how long you can stay up without staggering with your eyes open and with them closed. Try it with your eyes open but wearing a mask with small eye-holes. Does narrowing your field of view make it harder? What happens if you cross your eyes?

DRAWING IN A MIRROR

You can experience something a little bit like an upside-down world with a "mirror drawing" experiment (below). First draw a shape such as a star on a piece of paper. Now put the piece of paper in front of a mirror so that you can see its reflection. Next, hold a piece of card between you and the paper so that you can't see it directly, but can still see its reflection. Now for the hard part! Try to trace around the edge of the shape using the reflection of the shape and your hand in the mirror as your only guide. Keep trying a few times with new shapes, or words. You will find that you get steadily better at it as you learn to cope with the reversed visual world in the mirror.

Eye On The Ball

In some sports, you have to learn to use your eyes to hit, catch, kick or jump accurately.

WHEN YOU REACH for a door handle, catch a falling glass or jump over a puddle, your brain uses messages from your eyes to work out how far away things are from you and how fast they or you are moving. Then it sends the right commands to your muscles, so that you reach the right way, or jump the right distance. When you play ball games or other sports, you need to reach, catch and jump even more quickly and accurately.

By finding out how our brains use information from our eyes, scientists have discovered better ways of training athletes.

WHERE WILL IT FALL? ◀

When you are a fielder in a ball game such as rounders, how do you know where to run to catch the ball? If the ball is hit low, it's easy, but a ball hit high up into the sky is more difficult. Professional fielders learn to run into a position that would be directly under the ball if it were climbing straight up. When the ball drops, they are right underneath it. Next time you watch a ball game, watch the fielders running to catch balls. Do they look where they are going, or do they look at the ball?

RETURNING A SERVE ▼

When you play tennis or cricket, you have to swing the racquet or bat at exactly the right moment to hit a speeding ball. You also have to hit the ball in the right direction and for the right distance. To get it right, you must learn to control where you look. First keep your eye on the ball, then at just the right moment look at where you want the ball to go. The direction that your head and eyes are pointing is very important!

Brain Games

How many coins?

Bend your arm in the same way as in the picture (left) and balance a stack of coins on your elbow. How high can you make the stack before the coins fall off? While you're trying to balance them, keep your eyes on the stack so that you can see if it is wobbling. Once you've got a tall stack only just balanced, turn your head and look away. What happens? Is it just as easy to keep the coins balanced now?

Don't spill it!

Fill a glass full to the brim with water and walk around holding it (right). Keep it steady and don't spill any water. Now, try to do the same thing without looking at the glass. Can you still walk without spilling any water, or do you need to look at the glass to keep it steady? (Be sure to try this outdoors.)

One-handed juggling

Throw a ball up into the air a few times, and catch it in one hand (above). Now, try shutting your eyes while the ball is falling towards your hand. You'll find that you can catch the ball perfectly well with your eyes shut, provided you close them only just before you catch. If you close your eyes any sooner, you'll usually miss the ball. By switching the lights out while people catch balls, scientists have found that you have to be able to see the ball until three-tenths of a second before you catch it. After that, it doesn't matter whether you can see it or not!

Flip and catch

Put a small place-mat on the edge of a table, partly sticking out over the edge. Flick it into the air by bringing your hand up quickly underneath it (below), then try to catch it with the same hand before it lands again. Once you can do it every time, try it while looking away, or use several mats.

Long jumping

How do long jumpers hit the take-off board with one foot so accurately every time (below)? Find out by setting up your own long jump. (You don't have to jump to do this experiment.) You need a surface such as damp sand where you can see your footprints. Make a mark on the ground and run or walk towards it several times, each time bringing your foot right on to the mark. Measure the distances between your last 5–10 strides. How many strides back do you start to shorten or lengthen your pace? Most trained athletes start to adjust their pace three strides back — keeping their eyes on the take-off board as they run.

That Looks Familiar

Familiar sights — whether faces or objects — are easy to take for granted. What helps you identify them?

MOST OF THE TIME, you don't have any trouble telling what things are when you see them. But it can be more difficult when you see something from an unusual angle, or in a situation where you don't expect to see it. Your brain relies on things being in their usual places and positions to identify them quickly, without you having to puzzle over them. Something we're all especially good at is recognising other people's faces. When you think how little difference there is between one face and another, it is amazing that you can recognise hundreds or even thousands of different faces.

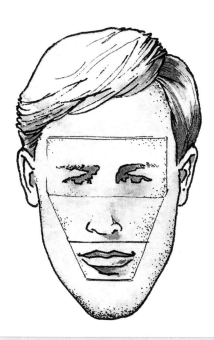

WANTED: THIS FACE

Identikit (Photofit) is used to help witnesses to crimes make a picture of the face of the person wanted by the police. The kit consists of lots of photographs of different mouths, noses, eyes, chins and hairlines, which fit together to make many different faces. The witness tries out combinations of these photographs to find the one that looks most like the face they remember.

Brain Games

GUESS WHO?

Whose face is in this drawing (left)? Take a good look before you turn the book upside-down to check. (If you are still puzzled, look on the Answers page.) Most things are equally easy to recognise either way up, but upside-down faces usually take a little longer to identify. This may be because from the time we are born we mostly see other people's faces when they are the right way up.

GUESS WHO AGAIN!

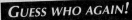

Who is this (right)? You probably cannot tell. But if you hold the picture away from you and screw up your eyes to blur your vision, you may be able to recognise the face? If you wear glasses or contact lenses, try it without them. The photograph has been processed by computer to divide it into small squares and make the colours run together. If you still cannot tell who it is, turn to the Answer page to find out.

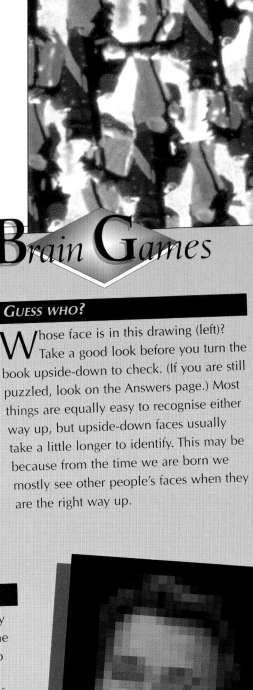

This picture looks like just a lot of triangles, squares and other coloured shapes, but it is a photograph of a real-life scene. There are several things that make it difficult to say what it is. First, the photograph is blurred. Secondly, it is upside-down. (If you turn the page upside-down you will see what it is immediately.) Also, all the people are marching close together, seeming to form one large pattern, so it is very difficult to pick out individual people and uniforms. Finally, there is no background to provide more clues.

A STRANGE FACE

What is peculiar about this face (left)? At first it looks like an upside-down picture of a normal face, but look carefully. (If you are not sure, check the Answers page.) You can make your own strange faces with pictures cut out of magazines.

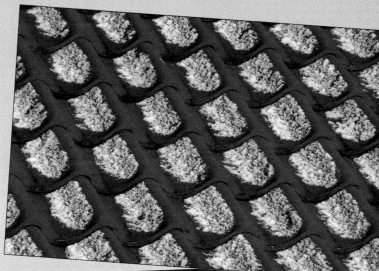

WHAT PLANET IS THIS?

Photographs taken from hundreds of miles out in space by satellites can be used to make maps of the surfaces of planets. This map (below) has been made from satellite photographs, but there is something slightly unusual about it that makes it different from most maps. Which planet do you think it shows? (A hint: if you discover what is unusual about it, that should tell you straight away which planet it is.) When you think you know, turn to the Answers page to check.

WHAT IS IT?

What are you looking at (above)? It is difficult to know because of the way the photograph has been taken. If you saw this scene in real life, you would know straight away what it was, because you would see all of its surroundings at the same time. Once you've made your best guess, turn to the Answers page to check.

Answers

SPOT THE MISTAKE   PAGE 17

COUNTING SIDES   PAGE 17

The answers are (from top down) 10, 8, 5 and 16.

COMPLETE THE PICTURE   PAGE 17

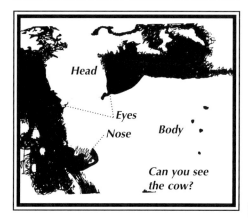

FIND THE SQUARE   PAGE 19

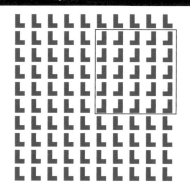

FIND THE ANIMALS   PAGE 21

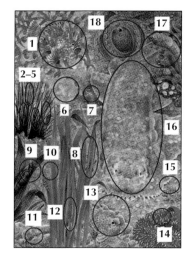

1. Sargassum fish; 2-5. Urchin shrimp fish; 6. Common jellyfish; 7. Starlet; 8. File fish; 9. Sea hare; 10. Aesop prawn; 11. Crab; 12. Shrimp fish; 13. Stone fish; 14. Clown fish; 15. Burrowing anemone; 16. Carpet shark; 17. Cling fish; 18. Octopus.

FALSE IDENTITY   PAGE 21

Clockwise from top right: a cricket imitating a leaf; a moth that looks like bark; a moth with "eyes" on its wings; a caterpillar imitating bird droppings; a hoverfly that looks like a wasp.

COLOURBLINDNESS   PAGE 23

The number in the circle is 67.

BEHIND THE SCENE   PAGE 27

The image is a horse.

IMPOSSIBLE PICTURE   PAGE 28

PHOTOGRAPHIC MEMORY   PAGE 36

How many deer are there in the picture? Are they the only large animals in the scene? Is the stream to the left or to the right of the trees? What time of year is it? How many geese are flying overhead? What is the landscape in the far background?

WHAT DID YOU SEE?   PAGE 37

GUESS WHO?   PAGE 42

The face belongs to Margaret Thatcher, former British Prime Minister.

GUESS WHO AGAIN!   PAGE 42

It's Arnold Schwarzenegger!

A STRANGE FACE   PAGE 43

The face is upside-down, but the eyes, nose and mouth are the right way up.

WHAT IS IT?   PAGE 43

Snow on the tiles of a rooftop.

WHAT PLANET IS THIS?   PAGE 43

Earth, as a mirror image, with the oceans (instead of the land) shown in detail.

Glossary

Binocular vision
Combining the images at the backs of your retinas to form a single view of the world.

Colourblindness
Not being able to tell some colours apart. Red-green colourblindness is most common, but blue-yellow colourblindness also exists.

Colour constancy
How the colours of things look the same to your eyes even though the colour of the light falling on them changes.

Complementary colour
The colour you see as an after-image of another colour. Blue and yellow are complementary to each other; so are red and green.

Cone
A type of cell in the retina which turns light into an electrical message.

Depth perception
Seeing the things around you as solid, and at different distances away from you.

Echolocation
Using the sound bouncing off objects to tell what they are and how far away they are.

Evolution
How living things, over many generations, come to be better adapted to their environments.

Five senses
Seeing, hearing, touch, smell and taste. (Smell and taste are linked.)

Focus
The way in which your eyes form an image to make it clear and sharp.

Fovea
A small area of your retina where vision for detail is especially good.

Infrared
Light with wavelengths longer than red light. It is invisible to people, but visible to some animals.

Lens
The part of the eye behind the iris and the pupil which bends light rays to form an image. It becomes thicker or thinner to bring the image into focus, according to whether the object is near or distant.

Light
A form of energy which travels very fast in straight lines called rays. The energy comes in "packets" a tiny distance apart. This distance is called the wavelength. Light with a long wavelength appears red to us. Shorter wavelengths appear as orange, yellow, green, blue, indigo and (the shortest) violet — in that order.

Optical illusion
A picture or object that plays tricks on your eyes, causing you to see something which is not really there, or something different from what is really there.

Perspective
The way that the layout of a real scene is expressed in the shape of a picture or image.

Primary colour
One of three colours that can be mixed in different combinations to produce other colours. Red, blue and green are the primary colours of light; red, blue and yellow are the primary colours of pigments. Mixing coloured light is different from mixing pigments because the colour of the pigment depends on the wavelengths of light absorbed by the pigment. If you mix red, blue and green paints you get dark grey, because the mixture absorbs all wavelengths to almost the same degree. But if you add red, green and blue light in the right proportions, you get white light.

Pupil
A circular opening just in front of the lens which allows light into your eye.

Retina
The layer of light-sensitive cells which covers the back of your eye.

Rod
A type of cell in the retina which turns light into an electrical message and can work in dim light.

Spectrum
The series of colours you see as light changes wavelength. The full spectrum is made up of red, orange, yellow, green, blue, indigo and violet.

Ultraviolet
Light with wavelengths shorter than violet light. It is invisible to people, but visible to some animals.

Virtual reality
A way of making television pictures change as you move about, in the same way as if you moved through a real scene.

Visualisation
Creating a "picture in your head" of an imaginary scene or object.

Wavelength
The tiny distance between two waves of energy in a ray of light. Wavelength determines colour: red has the longest wavelength, and violet has the shortest, with other colours in between.

Index